EVERY BEAR'S LIFE GUIDE

EVERY BEAR'S LIFE GUIDE

BRIDGID HERRIDGE
illustrated by Stephen Donovan

EBURY PRESS

Published by Ebury Press
National Magazine House
72 Broadwick Street
London W1V 2BP

First hardcover edition 1984

© Charles Herridge Ltd 1983

ISBN 0 85223 306 X

Produced by Charles Herridge Ltd., Tower House,
Abbotsham, Bideford, Devon.
Typeset by Toptown Printers Ltd, Barnstaple,
Devon.
Printed by BAS Printers Ltd, Over Wallop,
Hampshire.

FOREWORD

CALLING ALL TEDDY BEARS!

This book will totally transform your life!

For too long bears have been acceptors — accepting without protest all that life throws at them. Bears have traditionally been comforters — a sympathetic ear for the problems of others, a butt for their anger and frustrations, a shoulder to cry on.

But who takes notice of a bear's opinions? Who comforts a teddy when he's down. Nurses him when he's sick? Cherishes him when he's old? No one! Bears have been USED.

Being held in such low esteem by society it is little wonder that most bears have a very negative image of themselves — not surprising that they let themselves go, both mentally and physically.

Now all this is going to change. It is time for bears to bite the hand that feeds them and go out and grab their own vittles. It is time for bears to take responsibility for their own lives.

Every Bear's Life Guide will show you how to:

★ boost your self-confidence

★ look good and feel great

★ assert yourself and demand your rights

★ make lots of money

★ be a fulfilled bear

So forget your cuddly image, your gentle nature, your winning ways. You too can have it all — just barge in there and grab it.

BCTH, The Shed,
The Bottom of the Garden,
Abbotsham.

CONTENTS

ROOTS

Understanding Your Heritage

Without roots, a tree cannot grow; it withers and dies. And so it is with Bear. Bear has tried to cut himself off from his roots. Forgetting the proud traditions and simple faith of his forebears, he has attempted to graft himself on to unsuitable root stock, to live parasitically on others. But, by rejecting his past and accepting the false tenets of the modern world, he is in danger of losing his essential being, his true nature, his Bearness.

In order to understand his true nature every bear must go back to his roots. He must study the Origins of Bear and the rich heritage of his proud past. He must recall his evolution from humble draught excluder to that noble two-legged creature, primitive bear; he must marvel at his creation by that mysterious Sewing Machine in the Sky; he should look back to the days when bears were bears, free to roam the woodland paths, to hunt and fish in the forests and lakes of Mother Nature's Bear Garden; he should recall the great achievements of his illustrious ancestors. Bears can only regain their self-esteem and dignity if they reject the false roles assigned to them in today's world. They can only free themselves from their bondage if they return to the values of their forebears!

Be proud of your heritage and remember

FUR IS FABULOUS!

GROWLS ARE GLORIOUS!

CUBS ARE CUTE!

and

BEARS ARE THE BEST!

EVOLUTION

From Cushion to Future Bear

Where did bears come from? Bear as we know him has not existed on this earth for a very long period of time, but his predecessors may go back many hundreds of years. Most authorities now believe that the handsome, two-legged bear of today evolved from a single-celled organism — a speck of dust perhaps. Then gradually, through natural selection and survival of the fittest speck, cotton wool balls developed. We do not know exactly when the first soft furnishings appeared on earth, but they must have been very simple beings.

The Cushion

In the beginning was the Cushion. Not a very impressive object — simply a lump of padding material held together with some sort of covering — but from this inauspicious start developed two reptilian forms that were the direct ancestors of modern bear.

The Bean Bag Frog

One of the first evolutionary steps occurred when a mutant, mis-shapen Cushion was created. He must have appeared very strange to his fellow cushions, but he was the first Bean Bag Frog. Filled with beans, rice or other non-toxic substance, he had two eyes and four legs. Bean Bag Frogs, however, were pretty useless on land, being incredibly floppy, and in water they tended to sink.

The Draught Excluder

At about the same time as the Bean Bag Frog was emerging, the Cushion was developing along different lines into the Draught Excluder. At first merely a long thin Cushion, it gradually evolved eyes, a forked tongue and a patterned body. Its tendency to lie along the bottom of draughty doors perhaps points to the lack of an efficient body cooling mechanism.

The Toy Dog

From these rather basic creatures the first Toy Dog (*Canis crepundia*) developed. Long and thin like a Draught Excluder, and with four legs like a Bean Bag Frog, he still had difficulty in moving about owing to his very short appendages.

Dog-on-Wheels

Movement became easier with the

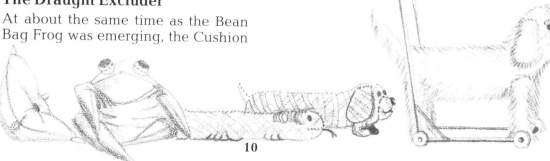

invention of the wheel. Dog-on-Wheels was a very successful species for many years but is now threatened with extinction. A few remain in captivity but they appear to have difficulty in reproducing themselves under these circumstances.

When the first soft toy stood up and walked on two legs instead of four, modern bear was born.

The Koala

The Koala *(Ursus australiensis)* is probably the earliest bear form, from which all the others have evolved. If left to their own devices Koalas tend to revert to rather primitive behaviour, but the belief that they are not as intelligent as other races has little foundation in fact.

The Panda

The Panda *(Ursus pekinensis)* is also a member of an ancient race, but is more cultured and subtler than the Koala. Remains of Pekin Bear have been found which prove that Pandas were living in tower block apartments when Koalas were still swinging through the trees.

The Teddy Bear

The Teddy Bear *(Ursus edwardii)* is now the predominant bear type. He can vary greatly in appearance but is generally an overall colour, usually light brown to ginger.

Future Bear

Who knows how evolution will change the appearance of bears in the future?

WAS GOD A SEWING MACHINE?

and Alternative Theories of Creation

Although most thinking bears now lean towards the evolutionary theory to explain how bears came to inhabit the earth, many other ideas have been put forward to explain the miracle of creation.

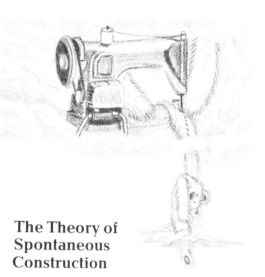

The Theory of Spontaneous Construction

Many bears are not prepared to believe that they evolved from a cushion. How could such complex, sensitive, intelligent beings develop from an old bag of feathers? Since ancient times bears have passed down legends of their creation by a mysterious being. He is known by various names in different parts of the world — "Pfaff", "Neff", "Eastman", "Singer" — but all these different racial religions have one common factor. The image of the sewing machine crops up in all the major religious groups and it has been suggested that this is a deeply rooted racial memory in every bear's subconscious, although its meaning is not clear. Some creationists believe that this god/sewing machine spontaneously created the first bear and they point to the marks of seams and stitching on our bodies to uphold this strange theory.

Extra-terrestrial Bears

Is bear an extra-terrestrial being? Some very convincing evidence has been put forward by Erich Von Furrykin, who maintains that the constellations Ursa Major and Ursa Minor were the original home of bears. He has found on a rock in his

back garden what he believes is a primitive illustration recording how a rocket ship came to earth from the Great Bear group of stars and left behind two of its crew of bears. We do not know if these bears were sent to colonize the earth or whether they just missed the last rocket home, but Von Furrykin believes they were the mother and father of all bears.

The Big Bang Theory

There are also those who believe that bear life was the result of a huge explosion of supernovae caused by the interaction of pulsars and quasars when subjected to the Doppler Effect and Hubble's Law. The dynamic energy so released injected life into the cosmic fibres suspended in the nebula, which were brought together by neutrino attraction to create bear as we know him. As nobody can understand this theory it is probably true.

FORE BEARS
The Search for the Lost Valley of the Teds

Bears have always believed that somewhere on this earth there still exists a tribe of noble savages, untouched by the evil influences of the modern world; that in some secret part of the globe bears still picnic in the sunshine, hunt in the forests and fish in the lakes, as did our prehistoric ancestors.

Many brave bears have died on fruitless expeditions to the outer reaches of civilization in their search for the Lost Valley of the Teds — the Utopia where they hope to recapture the true spirit of our past. Now, at last, the intrepid explorers Armand and Michaela Grizzleton-Tedham-Fiends have discovered this long-lost paradise. They have just returned from a year-long sojourn with the missing Teds, so proving, at last, that the legendary tribe really does exist.

Their latest book (*Westbound via Woodford*, Grizzley Books, £14.95) describes their terrifying journey up the infamous Ealing-Ongar Central Track and into the vast depths of Epping Forest. It was here, after

months of gruelling exploration through impenetrable undergrowth, that they came upon a magical sunlit valley the like of which they had only imagined in their wildest dreams.

Entering this paradise they were surrounded by a tribe of beautiful golden-furred bears, whose leader approached them boldly and gave them the traditional Ted "Hug". Naked except for his bear skin, his only adornment a bone through his nose, he was the epitome of the noble bear they were seeking.

Armand and Michaela spent many happy months with the Teds, studying their ancient civilization. Violence, disease, psychological disorders, home computers and house plants were almost unknown amongst them.

Polygamy was the rule and both sexes shared equally the hunting, cooking, hoovering and cubcare. The explorers were privileged to take part in the Teds' annual religious rites, which seemed to be based on ceremonial picnics in the woods where female priestesses led community singing.

When the day came for Armand and Michaela to leave the valley to return to the complex problems of the modern world, their hearts were heavy at parting from their new-found friends, whose idyllic lifestyle had shown them how our forebears had lived.

GREAT BEARS IN HISTORY
Your Illustrious Ancestors

Bears' influence on art, literature and world events has never been publicly recognized but the fact is — behind every great person or organization there is an even greater bear.

Pictured here: William Shakespeare; Teddy Roosevelt and his Rough Riders; Abraham Lincoln; Adolf Hitler; the Soviet Leadership.

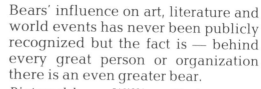

FITNESS WORKSHOP

Are You Fit to Live?

Fitness is the most important aspect of everybear's life, requiring constant attention at all times of day. Not a morsel of food must pass your lips until you have considered its value to your body or the strain it may place on your organs. Every movement you make should be thought of as an exercise to bring your body to peak physical condition. It is criminal for a bear to have lumps and bumps, to allow himself to become saggy and baggy. All it takes is 24-hour-a-day fitness plan.

Now is the time to start remoulding your body into a truly amazing, awe-inspiring creation. It is well worth spending most of the day toning up your personal powerhouse so that when you look in the mirror you can admire the wonderful specimen of bearhood that stares proudly back at you. And remember, UNLESS YOU LIVE FOR FITNESS YOU ARE NOT FIT TO LIVE!

Before you join our fitness workshop you must find out if you have enough puff. The graph shows how a typical bear breathes. You should complete such a chart each day. A break in the puff count line indicates that you have stopped breathing and are therefore not very fit.

The "Are You Breathing?" Chart

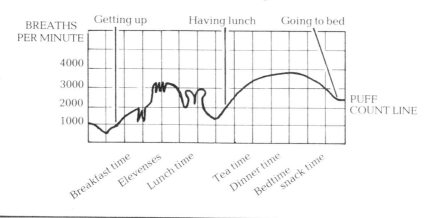

WELL BEAR CLINIC

Looking for Trouble

Most bears assume, just because they feel well, that they are quite healthy. This is a grave misconception. Really horrible things can be happening to your body without you realizing it. The price of fitness and health is constant vigilance and every day you should give yourself a complete physical check-up to make sure that you are not deteriorating.

Self-examination for Lumps

Coagulated stuffing has become one of the most prevalent disorders among middle-aged bears. Regular self-examination for lumps is a must.

The Pinch Test

A good stuffing pressure is essential for health. If you can pinch an inch you should start worrying about the state of your filling.

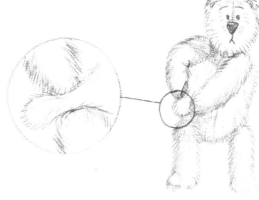

Seam Tension Probe

Weak seams are the beginning of the end healthwise and a daily seam tension probe is recommended.

ARE YOU WELL?

It is well worth spending a few hours each day checking your body for signs of deterioration. Stand in front of a full-length mirror and work through the checklists below.

WELL BEAR CHECKLIST

Answer yes or no (truthfully) to the following questions.

1 Are your ears firm and upstanding?
Yes ☐ No ☐
2 Are your eyes bright and shiny?
Yes ☐ No ☐
3 Is your nose cold and damp?
Yes ☐ No ☐
4 Do you have thick glossy fur?
Yes ☐ No ☐
5 Are your arms strong and well attached? Yes ☐ No ☐
6 Are your seams tight and strong?
Yes ☐ No ☐
7 Is your body firm and rounded?
Yes ☐ No ☐
8 Do you have strong chubby legs?
Yes ☐ No ☐
9 Are your feet perfectly formed?
Yes ☐ No ☐

If you can answer yes to all these questions you are a healthy bear. If you give two or more "no" answers go on to the Sick Bear Checklist.

VERY SICK BEAR CHECKLIST

1 Do you only have one ear?
Yes ☐ No ☐
2 Are your eyes falling out?
Yes ☐ No ☐
3 Is there a hole where your nose used to be? Yes ☐ No ☐
4 Are you going bald? Yes ☐ No ☐
5 Do you have any arms missing?
Yes ☐ No ☐
6 Are your seams gaping?
Yes ☐ No ☐

7 Is your body lumpy and sagging?
Yes ☐ No ☐
8 Do your legs give way under you?
Yes ☐ No ☐
9 Do any of your feet face backwards?
Yes ☐ No ☐

EVALUATION

If you answer "yes" to any of these questions you should seriously consider a change in your lifestyle and adopt the helpful advice in the following pages. Three or more "yes" answers indicate more serious medical problems and you should consult your doctor before joining our Fitness Workshop.

K-POK DIET

Our bodies are made up of approximately 95% fibre. Busy bears wear out this stuffing very fast. It is therefore essential that this fibre is replaced regularly if we are to keep fit and healthy.

The latest medical research shows that the lack of fibre in the diet of Western Bear is the cause of many of the ailments so prevalent in bear society today — general lethargy, abdominal prolapse, coagulation of the stuffing, weakness of the axillary and inguinal seams, can all be caused by lack of fibre.

Now, for the first time, nutrition experts have devised a revolutionary new diet that can prevent and cure all these and many other bear disorders. If you follow our phenomenal K-Pok Diet you will experience an explosion of well-being; a New You will emerge — strong, fit, healthy and raring to go.

Kapok — The Wonder Food

Our eating plan is based on kapok. This natural fibre source, which in recent years has been neglected by Western Bear, who prefers the convenience of man-made substitutes, turns out to be a wonder food! When combined with other fibre sources it provides the balanced diet that can transform you into a Superbear.

FIBRE FILLER

The most important part of your dieting day will be your bucket of our explosive FIBRE FILLER. Every morning you must mix together the following ingredients in a large bucket (or small dustbin).

8 pawfuls	natural kapok
7 pawfuls	Arabian horsehair
6 pawfuls	whole new wool
5 pawfuls	surgical cotton wool
4 pawfuls	desiccated rags
3 pawfuls	foam fubber chunks
A pinch of	eider feathers

Stir the ingredients well, as the horsehair tends to sink to the bottom of the bucket, and EAT. If you can't manage a whole bucket in one sitting try eating a pawful now and then during the day — but remember you MUST eat all your FIBRE FILLER.

Other meals should also contain fibre-rich foods. Plan your menu around the delicious selection featured in our easy-to-follow Fibre Chart.

WHERE TO FIND YOUR FIBRE CHART

All entries in this chart are placed in order of merit using the

$$\text{equation} \quad \frac{\text{specific gravity}}{\text{volume}} \times \frac{\text{mass}}{\text{area}} = X$$

Item	% fibre weight for area	average serving	grams per unit × area
KAPOK *raw*	29.4	1 porridge bowl	10.0
boiled	24.8	3 ladles	10.0
steamed	92	9 egg cups	10.0
HORSEHAIR			
Arabian, *raw*	14.8	2 sacks	9.0
boiled	6½	10 5ml spoons	9.0
Knackers'	10.2	3 dollops	9.0
WOOL *pure new*	9.5	1 skein	8.0
recycled	3.0	¼ jumper	8.0
COTTON WOOL see WOOL			
RAGS *desiccated*	8.7½	3 oz	7.0
fresh	7.3	4.22 g	7.0
FOAM RUBBER CHUNKS	4.2	1 carrier bag	6.0
FEATHERS eider	2.1	3	5.0
hen	1.1	2	4.0
crow	0.1	1	3.0

CONTD p94

A TYPICAL DAY'S EATING ON THE K-POK DIET

7.30 ½ bucket Fibre Filler

Breakfast Scrambled foam rubber chunks
Toasted whole wool bread

11.30 ¼ bucket Fibre Filler

Lunch Kapok sandwich with horse
hair and mango chutney

3.30 ¼ bucket Fibre Filler

Dinner Chilli con Kapok on a bed of
whole brown feathers

Bedtime If you are still hungry make up
another bucket of Fibre Filler

DOCTOR'S WARNING:
The K-Pok Diet may cause a
certain amount of embarrassment
and discomfort during the early
weeks. Do *not* be put off by this.
The results are worth it!

23

PUMPING FLUFF

Bulking Up and Getting Hard the Schwarzentedder Way

Do you want to look like Arnold Schwarzentedder, the world famous muscle bear? Do you yearn for the bulk and cuts of the Superchamp? If you want to be rugged and fit and massively muscled, then now's your chance — Arnold is prepared to let you, yes you, into his innermost training secrets . . .

"First you gotta bulk up your food intake. You gotta fill yourself up so full of stuffing that you can't squeeze in another strand of kapok or another granule of polystyrene. You gotta get all your body parts thoroughly congested. Food is the basic body building material, 'cos you can't shape up nothing. There are lots of good special muscle foods on the market but I use O'Growler's Patent Concentrated Freeze-dried Horsehair, boosted up with Queenie's Royal

Jelly when I'm preparing for an International Posedown.

"Once you got all the raw materials inside you you gotta get to work pumping all that fluff into the right places. It gives me a really fantastic high working that fluff into my abs, lats and delts. I myself personally favour the Heavy Duty Squat Roll Curl and the Hardcore Lat-Spread Enhancer. They gave me the real high-density rippled muscles that put me in the condition what I'm in today".

WARNING!

Arnold is a highly skilled body builder. When he over-pumps his delts like this he is able to extricate his head with his powerful arms. You may not be so lucky!

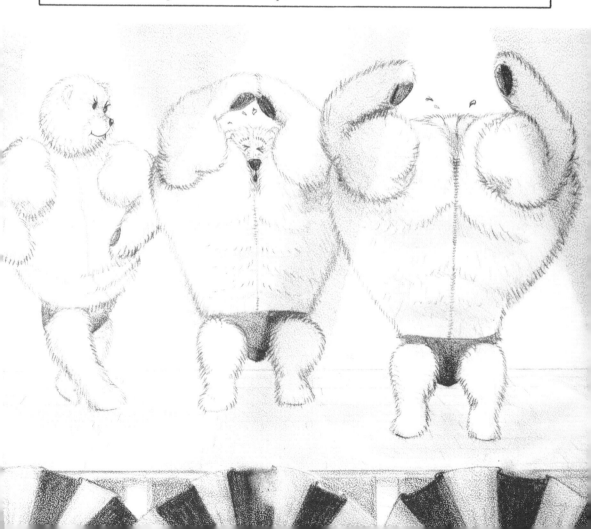

JANE PANDA'S WORKOUT

Bearobics for Beginners

Hi, I'm Jane Panda and I want to tell you how The Jane Panda Workout can help you attain beauty, health, success and wealth, while also freeing the world from disease, pollution, crime and war (and, incidentally, reversing the recession and bringing down the interest rate).

Although I lead an incredibly active and busy life I manage to set aside several hours each day for My workout and I find that this, together with a seven mile run, keeps Me in peak condition in both body and mind. If you want to look as fantastic as Me you must be prepared to dedicate yourself to My program with heart and soul!

My system is based on bearobics. Bearobics introduces air into your stuffing, so promoting a smooth, soft body (and a long life). This is done by drinking bearated mineral water, suffering unbearable pain and expelling a lot of hot air.

All you need to start My workout program are Jane Panda Leotards*, Jane Panda Leg Warmers*, Jane Panda Sweatbands*, Jane Panda records and tapes*, The Jane Panda Workout Book and, as these are almost impossible to follow without personal instruction, a two-year course at the Jane Panda Body Workshop.

So hurry along and join up right away before my prices go through the roof!

*Available at your local Jane Panda Shop.

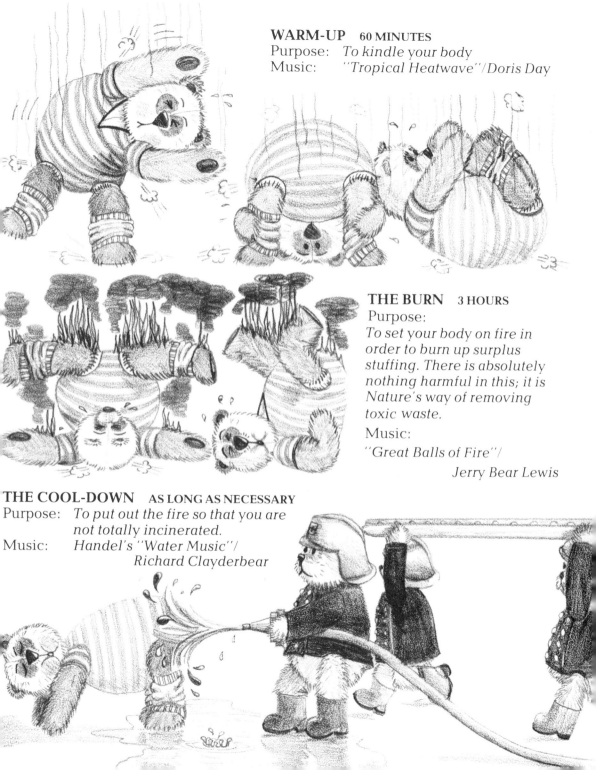

WARM-UP 60 MINUTES
Purpose: *To kindle your body*
Music: *"Tropical Heatwave"/Doris Day*

THE BURN   3 HOURS
Purpose:
*To set your body on fire in
order to burn up surplus
stuffing. There is absolutely
nothing harmful in this; it is
Nature's way of removing
toxic waste.*
Music:
"Great Balls of Fire"/
                Jerry Bear Lewis

THE COOL-DOWN   AS LONG AS NECESSARY
Purpose: *To put out the fire so that you are
            not totally incinerated.*
Music: *Handel's "Water Music"/
            Richard Clayderbear*

HEALTH AND FITNESS SUPERSTORE

Introducing the sensational NEW

SHRINK-MAC

SHRINK those unsightly OPEN PORES
and stop Fibre Loss!
with this amazing new PLASTIC
MACKINTOSH

The SHRINK-MAC builds up incredible heat and moisture underneath its stylish folds, which actually shrink those open pores so that your insides stay in where they're supposed to be!

Wear it while hoovering, pruning the roses, making a cup of tea — and let the MAC work on your pores.

Try it in the privacy of your own home on our 5 year "no risk" guarantee.

Universal Size — Fits Everybear

Airtight collar

Moist pockets

BODY HEAT BUILDS UP AND CIRCULATES

Velcro tastening

Drawstring hem for extra heat build-up

SEND NOW FOR YOUR SHRINK-MAC
To Paddington Products
The Station
London WX1 AB10 ZQY 7NT

Yes, I want to experience all the benefits of a SHRINK-MAC. Please send me .... Shrink-Macs at the low, low price of £59.75. I enclose the munny.
Love ....

PATENT PENDING   DIRECT FROM THE U.S. OF A.

MIRACLE STRING

The Complete Home Exercise System

This versatile piece of string is all you need for your complete home gym.

KNOT   it in a circle to exercise your fingers with a cat's cradle

WRAP   it round the door knob to develop your arms

TIE   it to your feet to flatten your tummy and hone down your thighs

SAVE!

TOP QUALITY STRING

originally £51-33

NOW ONLY

£14-95
plus VAT plus P&P
£51-35

This is an opportunity you cannot afford to miss

Send your money now to:
Brumas Health Products   Forest of Dean, Gloucs.

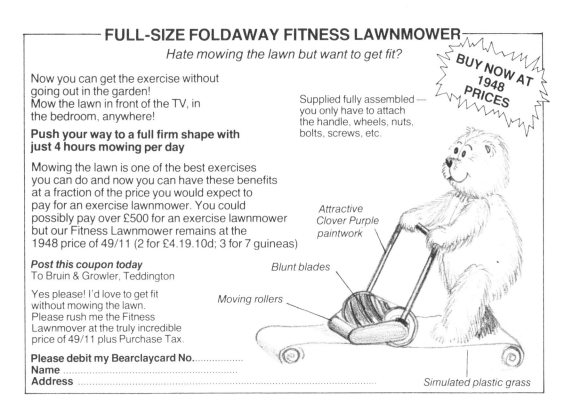
29

BEAR BEAUTIFUL
The Search for Perfection

A truly beautiful bear exudes an aura of serenity and inner strength. He is full and firm and soft to the touch. His fur is thick and glossy and glows with deep-down cleanliness. His symmetrical features and perfectly formed hands and feet cannot be faulted. Clothes to match his mood and style complete the devastating picture.

Of course, all this doesn't just come about by itself — it costs a great deal of time and money — but that wonderful feeling of knowing you are looking your best, those admiring glances that follow you everywhere, that truly wonderful bear who greets you from the mirror each morning, make the effort involved a pleasure rather than a chore. Your face and your body are your greatest assets and if you pamper them they could be your passport to the good life — they could lift you from the doldrums of a boring existence on to new planes of pleasure, success and romance.

THE BEAUTY GAME

Knowing All the Wrinkles

Deep Down Clean

The secret of beauty lies in scrupulous cleanliness. Regular deep cleansing is essential. There have been arguments in recent years over the merits of handwashing versus the automatic washing machine, and natural drying versus the tumble dryer. A healthy bear need not fear the advances of modern technology. Used with care such beauty aids will only enhance your looks. It has to be admitted that accidents have occurred with some of these machines where unscrupulous or untrained operatives have used incorrect temperatures or wash cycles.

However, in the hands of professional beauticians using British Standard equipment and high quality cleansers, automatic deep cleansing should cause no problems.

When making an appointment for deep cleansing you should specify a "delicates" or "wool" programme if you want to play safe. In certain circumstances, for instance if you have a problem with enlarged pores through which stuffing oozes on occasions, a "whites" or "colour-fast" cycle may be recommended. This treatment can shrink the pores, although you may find it plays havoc with your fur. It is also a good idea to

ask for a fabric conditioner to be added to your final rinse for that really luxurious, deep softness.

Of course, if you really want to pamper yourself you could splurge out on a dry cleaning treatment with optional retexturing, but take care to stay in well-ventilated places for a few days afterwards or you may find yourself or your friends overcome by fumes.

Hand washing in a non-allergenic soap product produces good results but great care must be taken to remove all the cleanser. Those embarrassing sudsy emissions that can occur in rainstorms may be due to inadequate rinsing.

Bright Eye Tips

A bear's eyes should be limpid pools. A useful tip for keeping them shiny is to relax with tissues soaked in Windolene over your eyes. After ten minutes rub your eyes gently and they'll gleam like newly polished mirrors.

In a hurry? then try a bit of spit and polish for a quick eye buff.

The Secret of Eternal Youth

A major tell-tale sign of approaching old age are those little bald patches that begin to appear on your body. When they can no longer be disguised with the discreet use of felt-tipped pen, it is time to consider body wigs. Very realistic fur pieces can be purchased these days, but you must be careful to match your fur colour exactly. Nothing looks worse than a red-tinged toupée on a brown-furred bear!

Fur pieces can merely be glued over the balding area or they can be stitched on in a simple operation requiring only a local anaesthetic. Fur transplants, where whole areas of the epidermis are replaced by new skin and fur, are more complex operations and should only be undertaken by fully qualified fur surgeons.

COSMETIC SURGERY

The Fight Against Decay

No bear's perfect and as we get older our imperfections become more noticeable. That eye that was slightly higher than the other, those oddly placed ears, that crooked nose, look worse on a mature Ted whose stuffing is deteriorating and whose skin is beginning to sag. But why put up with these imperfections and this bodily decay? Today's bear must be as aggressive in the fight against the ravages of time as in all other aspects of life.

A sagging face or body can be pumped up again to the full, round firmness of youth by acrylic fibre shots. A course of these injections is expensive and time-consuming but the results are worth the inconvenience — unless of course your body is allergic to man-made fibres and rejects the implant. This can be rather a messy business. Although natural cotton wool can be used as a substitute, this tends to become compressed in time and is not as long lasting.

Sagging can be caused by stretched skin as well as stuffing deterioration, and in these cases it is advisable to have a face and abdomen lift as well as a fibre implant. In mild cases a hot steam shrink may suffice but sometimes an operation to take in the seams or remove the excess skin may be required.

Eye, ear and nose shifts are available for those bears born with asymmetrical features and are also advisable after a face lift.

Bears who have been disfigured in accidents or who were always

"imperfect" or "seconds", as they say, can usually obtain treatment under the Medibear Service if they are prepared to wait. Bears in a hurry or with less serious defects who have financial problems may find a surgeon prepared to accept easy terms or to allow you to wash up his instruments after operations in lieu of payment.

Just remember, you don't have to accept what Mother Nature gave you. In the search for your ultimate bear potential you must even be prepared to "go under the scissors".

WARNING:

When choosing a surgeon for your cosmetic operation make sure that his is a fully trained Bear Enchancement Specialist. Unscrupulous operators can cause untold damage and may not have the skill to put you back together properly. Reputable surgeons are fed up with being asked to undo the work of these cowboys.

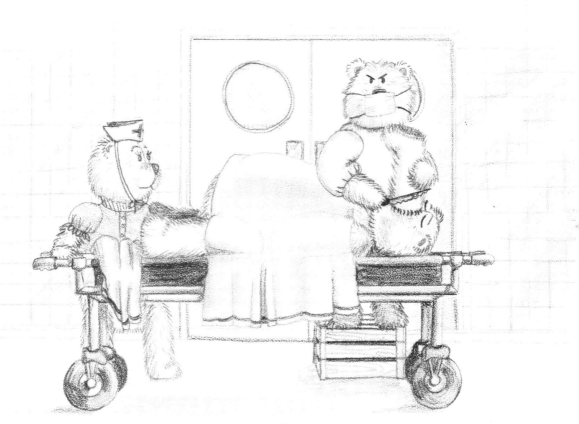

FIND YOUR STYLE

Off-the-Peg Identities

When it comes to clothes, it is essential that you find a style that not only enhances your beauty but expresses your personality and aspirations. Here we supply you with some off-the-peg personalities.

On the left. Barry poses in the ever-so-current **artisan** outfit — casual and practical and OK at today's fashion-able gatherings. Contrasting, but useful if you want to get ahead is the unisex **executive** style — crisp, tidy and unobtrusive. Executive leisure-wear is equally boring.

A perennial favourite is the **French Impressionist,** much beloved of weekend bohemians and jetset interior decorators. Painting skills are

not essential but the bit sticking out of the top of the beret absolutely is. And if this isn't unconventional enough for you then **Knight of the Road** it has got to be. This is strictly for summer wear though; when winter comes executive and Sloane styles are warmer.

You don't have to be a **student** to dress like one, but if you can get a grant, rooms in college and hot meals in hall, life is a bed of roses. And there are endless opportunities for political agitation and Ted Lib sit-ins.

Used car salesbears and bears who sell cheap watches in pubs will find the customers flocking to them if they dress like **medallion bear** here, for this is the correct attire of their calling. Impressively casual and devil-may-care, it nevertheless speaks volumes about you. Gold identity bracelet, gold watch, gold-style rings and gold buckles on belt and shoes complete the picture.

These accessories are absolutely out if you want to be a **Sloane bear,** whose style is muted and whose clothes are well-worn. This is the one for suburban bears wanting to look like country landowners, though ownership of a rebellious and exotic-looking **punk youth** may make this difficult.

New Age Bear is responsible for his own health. Armed with our 8-point Plan for eternal life, our Totally Unique Self Diagnosis Chart, our Encyclopedia of Illness and our Explicit Medical Drawings, you will possess in your own home a complete reference library which will enable you to avoid all life-threatening substances, monitor your worrying symptoms and cure all your diseases.

Everybear's 8-Point Plan for Eternal Life

1 *Do NOT eat or drink anything that has not been thoroughly tested by rats.* Feed your rat 2 cwt of your chosen substance over a 24 hour period and, if he appears to suffer no ill effects, it is probably safe for you to eat it.

2 *Beware of water.* Not only may water be polluted and unsafe to drink but soft water causes heart disease and hard water furs up your insides. Water is also the commonest cause of drowning.

3 *Avoid light.* The latest scientific research has revealed that, in a study of bears who had contracted FFS (Fading Fur Syndrome), 99% had been exposed to sunlight or artificial light at some time during their lives.

4 *Keep off the roads.* Road accidents are the commonest cause of accidental sudden death. Lead poisoning can also result from contact with motor vehicles.

5 *Stay out of the kitchen,* and avoid the home. Most other accidents occur in the home and the kitchen appears to be the most dangerous room in the house followed by badly lit stairs (but see point 3). It would seem that the less time spent at home the longer you are likely to live.

6 *Avoid electricity* — static or moving. It is believed that electricity from pylons, cables, air conditioners, TVs, man-made fibres, etc, reduces the ions in the air, causing headaches and fatigue (see point 8).

7 *Don't play games with your health.* Games and sports of all types have claimed many lives. Every day we read in the newspaper "Bear dies on Fun Run", "Footballer Injured", "Famous Sportsbear Dies". Sporting activity can damage your health.

8 *Get out of Bed.* 99% of all bears die in the prone position, and the majority of these in bed. Avoid any activity that may cause fatigue necessitating a lie down.

ENCYCLOPEDIA OF ILLNESS

An A-Z of Ailments — their prevention and cure

ABDOMINAL PROLAPSE

Abdominal prolapse or "dropped tum" is an occupational hazard of dentists and hairdressers and those whose jobs entail too much standing around. In the most serious cases the stomach can drop right down into the legs but a low-slung paunch below a weedy chest is the usual result. Tight trousers and hand stands can afford some relief.

ACCIDENTAL AMPUTATION

If you are unfortunate enough to lose a limb or other important part of your body remember to retain the detached appendage in a safe place as it is sometimes possible to re-attach the part and restore at least some of its function. Limb transplants from donors are never as successful and can look distinctly odd.

ACNE, BOILS AND CARBUNCLES

These are small skin lesions through which stuffing can escape. Never attempt to squeeze or pull out the offending matter. It is far better to push it back in and seal the hole in some way. Some bears like to rub polyunsaturated margarine on their boils.

ALOPECIA

Fur loss is a chronic condition of older bears which was once thought to be caused by wear and tear, though recent studies indicate that cholesterol may be involved. It is possible that when saturated fats get into your follicles your fur just slips out of the holes.

ANAEMIA

An overall lack of fibre usually caused by an inadequate diet or fibre loss through some lesion in the body. Symptoms include general lethargy, weakness and bandy legs. A low-cholesterol K-pok Diet can help and surgery to close up the lesions may be recommended.

ANOREXIA

An exciting new disease originally found only among naughty middle-class cubolescents who wouldn't eat up their roughage. However, it appears to be very contagious and anyone can get it now — from the lowest ted to the highest royal bear. Some sources suggest you can catch it from infected slimming magazines and diet books but it is probably caused by cholesterol.

ATHLETE'S FOOT

One of the many hideous side-effects of sport, which can wear away the soles of the feet. If left untreated these openings can lead to serious stuffing loss *(Flufforrhage)* and consequent *Anaemia.*

COAGULATION OF THE STUFFING

Coagulated stuffing is often the result of a diet rich in polyesterates. Some polyesters (especially cheap foreign imports) tend to matt and form fluff balls in the stomach which can move around the body causing unsightly fibre lumps. Treatment consists of surgical removal followed by a strict regime of polyunesterates.

DETACHED RETINA

Your eyeballs can fall out for any number of reasons — weak eye ligaments, overstretched skin, accident, old age or violence. Always make sure that eyes are well attached before you go out and have regular check-ups with your optician. Although eyes can be replaced the results are not always perfect and you could end up with a lop-sided squint.

FLUFFORRHAGE

When serious flufforrhage occurs, i.e. when stuffing pours uncontrollably out of your body, emergency action must be taken. Every bear should learn how to apply a tourniquet.

Applying a tourniquet

Tie a hanky above
the leaking area.

Insert stick . . .

and twist

Arrange for surgery as soon as possible.

HERNIATION OF THE STUFFING

A hernia or rupture is the protrusion of your insides onto the outside. This painful condition can be caused by strain, so avoid over-straining your axillary and inguinal seams. Obesity and cholesterol can also play a part. Surgical repair is the only real answer to the problem but some bears prefer to keep their insides in with a truss.

TOTAL ALLERGY SYNDROME

Some poor bears find that they are totally allergic to Life on Earth — they just fall apart when exposed to it. It is possible that they are extra-terrestrial bears and ought to go back to Ursa Minor or wherever they came from.

WHERE DOES IT HURT?

Totally Unique Self-Diagnosis Chart

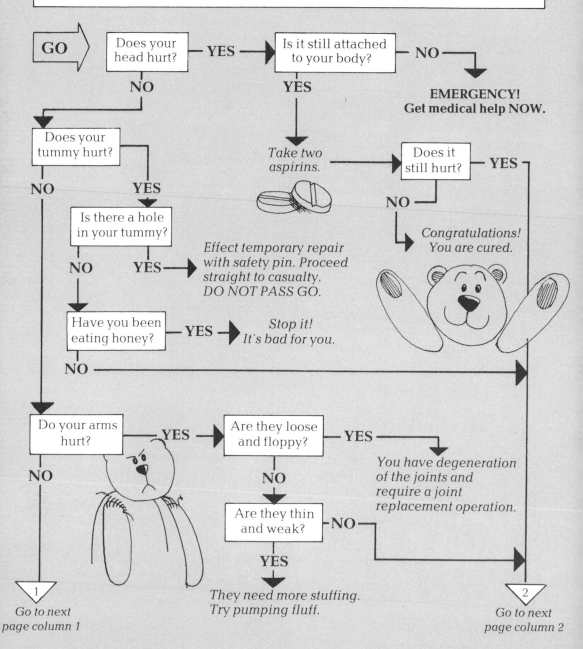

GO

Does your head hurt? — **YES** → Is it still attached to your body? — **NO** → **EMERGENCY! Get medical help NOW.**

NO

YES

Take two aspirins. → Does it still hurt? — **YES**

NO → Congratulations! You are cured.

Does your tummy hurt?

NO   **YES**

Is there a hole in your tummy?

NO   **YES** → *Effect temporary repair with safety pin. Proceed straight to casualty. DO NOT PASS GO.*

Have you been eating honey? — **YES** → *Stop it! It's bad for you.*

NO

Do your arms hurt? — **YES** → Are they loose and floppy? — **YES** → *You have degeneration of the joints and require a joint replacement operation.*

NO

NO

Are they thin and weak? — **NO**

YES

They need more stuffing. Try pumping fluff.

1

Go to next page column 1

2

Go to next page column 2

42

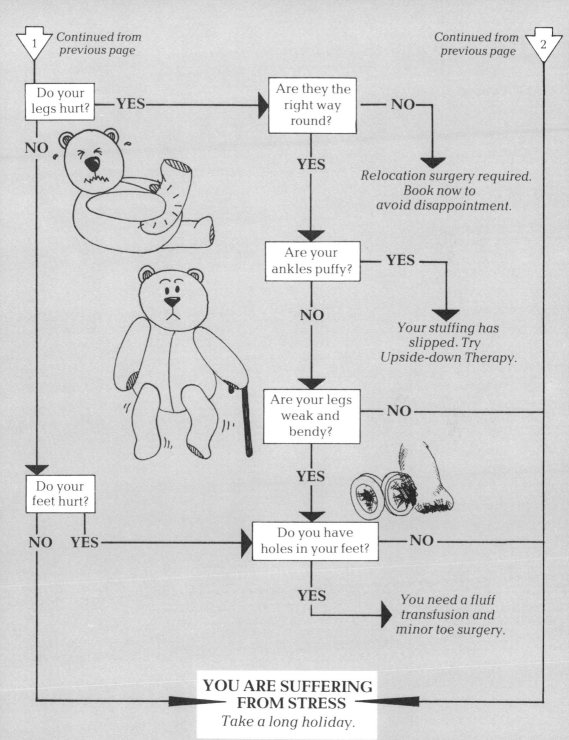

①
Continued from
previous page

Continued from
previous page
②

Do your
legs hurt? —**YES**——————→ Are they the
right way
round? —**NO**——

NO

YES

Relocation surgery required.
*Book now to
avoid disappointment.*

Are your
ankles puffy? —**YES**——

NO

*Your stuffing has
slipped. Try
Upside-down Therapy.*

Are your legs
weak and
bendy? —**NO**——

YES

Do your
feet hurt?

NO **YES**———————→ Do you have
holes in your feet? —**NO**——

YES

*You need a fluff
transfusion and
minor toe surgery.*

**YOU ARE SUFFERING
FROM STRESS**
Take a long holiday.

EXPLICIT MEDICAL DRAWINGS

THESE PAGES CONTAIN
EXPLICIT MEDICAL
DRAWINGS WHICH MAY
CAUSE DISTRESS TO SOME
READERS. *SORRY.*

Here we have a sad case of INGROWN NOSE. This can be caused by a blow to the proboscis or abnormal pressure on the face.

This dentist is suffering from ABDOMINAL PROLAPSE. He was advised to change his employment and fitted with a pair of National Health trousers.

DETACHED RETINA is a normal part of the ageing process but can also occur in younger bears either as a congenital weakness of the eye ligaments or as a result of accidental damage to the optic nerve.

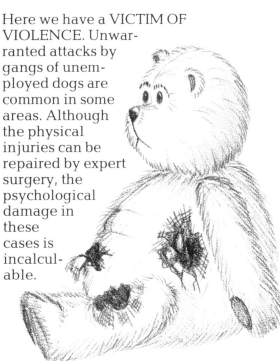

An elderly patient with severe ALOPECIA. This patient's illness has gone too far to be corrected by fur transplants but, from the look of him, the problem is unlikely to worry him for much longer.

Here we have a VICTIM OF VIOLENCE. Unwarranted attacks by gangs of unemployed dogs are common in some areas. Although the physical injuries can be repaired by expert surgery, the psychological damage in these cases is incalculable.

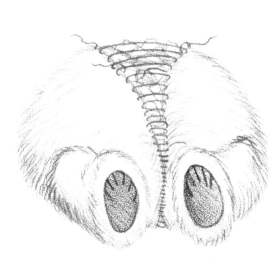

Obesity can cause VENTRAL RUPTURE. This patient will be fitted with a truss until his weight is reduced, when a surgical repair will be possible.

ON THE COUCH

Are You Mental?

The strain of living in the modern world is bound to take its toll on your mental well-being. Having taken steps to combat your physical degeneration, it is time to probe your mental health.

The following quiz will highlight just how mental you are. Once you know this you should be able to channel your insanity into useful, productive activities. Part I of the questionnaire is designed to show how much strain you are under. Part II will determine how it is affecting your mind.

Part I Are You Over-stressed?

In the following list tick the questions to which you would answer "yes".

a Do you have to get up every morning?
b . . . and brush your teeth?
c Are you forced to make conversation at breakfast?
d Are you required to show up at work most days?
e Are you tired and worn out most nights?

If you answer "yes" to more than one of these questions you are very likely to be suffering from stress. To find out if you are mental go on to Part II.

Part II Are You Mental?

Circle the answers below which apply to you.

1 When you wake up in the morning do you feel like
A a bear with a sore head? B a cup of tea? C Napoleon?

2 Do you think you are being cheated by
A the milkman? B your spouse? C the vicar?

3 Do you have a phobia about
A slugs? B bluebottles? C tapioca?

4 Are you obsessed by
A yourself? B your beer mat collection? C overmanning on the Bosphorus Ferry?

5 Do you have fantasies about
A money? B exotic beer mats? C the bear next door?

Evaluation

C answers indicate that you have a well balanced, integrated personality; B, that you are mildly deviant; A, that you are truly mental. If you are mental, do not worry, just turn to the next page.

STRESS YOURSELF UP
You've Got Somewhere to Go

STOP PRESS: Stress is good for you. Forget all that old hat about relaxation and leisure — Dr Ephraim Zimblebear has just discovered that the missing ingredient in most bears' lives is STRESS. All that lying about on beds could be the death of you, so wake up, get up, and get stressed!

Stress gets the adrenalin pumping, the heart beating, the pupils dilating — let stress be your "speed" for the 1980s!

There are 101 different ways to have a stress-making experience.

Why not try

The Traffic Jam
(or *La Confiture de Circulation* as they say on the Paris Périphérique). You'll always be able to find a snarl-up near you for a minor stimulant but for real high-level stress try the M5 on a summer Bank Holiday or the Autoroute at the end of July. Ten-mile tailbacks can do wonders for your adrenalin production.

48

Housebear Stress — the Family Way

One little tedling isn't really enough for the stress-seeking housebear. Try four or five. And remember, four or five little pre-school cublets may seem like the ultimate in stress, but just wait until they grow up into hulking great cubolescents. Yes, multiple cubbirth is the answer for those seeking really long-term stress.

Stress through crime

Breaking the law can be really exciting and gets the nerves a-tingling. Hiding in the cupboard under the stairs while the TV Detector van goes by; walking the dog at midnight, knowing you've not bought him a licence; parking on a single yellow line when no bear is looking — all these can bring back that added zest to life. If you need to up your stress dose after a while you could try planning a little petty larceny, but don't let things get out of hand or you may experience "convict stress".

Executive Stress

The secret of executive stress is telephones — lots and lots of them. They don't have to be real ones. Toy telephones with timing devices to make them ring at frequent intervals will do. Place them on a large executive desk, with all your executive pens, pencils, toys and papers and wait for the phone to ring.

HONEY DEPENDENCY

The True Story of a Bruin's Ruin

(Mr B is portrayed by an actor but his story is true).

We first interviewed Mr B at the Chorley Wood Destickification Centre where he was undergoing treatment for chronic hunniholism. His sad story is typical of the downhill slide that can occur when social honey-taking leads to a lonely honey-craving.

Mr B Speaks:

I was a rep for a well-known honey company. I used to eat a jar or two with the clients, nothing more; I could take it or leave it. Everything was fine till the '73 Honey Glut when the EEC Honey Lake caused the bottom to fall out of the market. I couldn't sell the stuff anywhere. I was worried, I can tell you!

It was then that I discovered that eating honey helped me forget my problems. When I started secret midnight honey raids the wife left me. By the time sales improved I found I couldn't stop. I lost my job when they found me eating the samples.

I eventually ended up on Sticky Row with all the other hunniholics. We used to take anything we could get our hands on — white sugar, saccharine, even cyclamates. That's where Brother Brumas found me. He persuaded me to come to this destickification centre and now I'm off the honey completely.

Who are the Guilty Bears?

Most bears enjoy a jar of honey and there is nothing wrong with that. It's when social eating develops into "honey abuse" that the problems start. Hunniholism is on the increase and the blame can be laid fairly and squarely at the door of the MEDIA. Books, TV and advertisements portray honey taking, and even honey abuse, as lovable and endearing traits. Famous and influential bears, whom young teds are inclined to take as role models, are pictured moving heaven and earth to get at the honey. Mentioning no names, a certain Mr P. . h (who also goes under the name of "Sanders") and a Mr Y. . i of Jellystone Park are particularly offensive in this way.

Let us hope that Mr B's sad tale will teach those young teds who are tempted to dip into the honeypot that honey can leave a sour taste.

BATTERED BEARS
The Vicious Triangle

Bear battering is not a pleasant subject but the facts have to be faced — bears are constantly being attacked by husbands, wives, children, dogs, cats, hamsters, in fact everyone seems to have it in for bears.

But why should this be? Is there some fault in bears themselves that invites such violence? Do we, in some way, ask to be battered? Some psychologists have suggested that it is our passive nature that encourages batterers to batter us. Perhaps, because we do not stand up for ourselves or answer back, we are attacked in order to produce some sort of reaction.

Whether or not this is the case, the tragic cycle of bear battering is a vicious triangle. A battered bear eventually becomes a tattered bear (see explicit batteree photographs opposite); tattered bears become rejected bears; rejected bears are battered. But how can we break the triangle and save bears from this degrading situation?

We asked Bearin Pizza-Eater, founder of the Battered Bear Movement and wife of *Playschool* star Little Ted. Bearin knows a lot about battering and how to deal with it. "You won't catch my Ted battering me" quipped the jolly bear from the ample folds of her all-enveloping kaftan as she patted her spouse on the head. "No, seriously though" she continued, "if you are a batteree, try battering your batterer back. If you're no good at battering, remove yourself from the battering situation and become a refugee batteree. Join other batterees in a Batteree Refuge where you can battle with the problems of battering, take Battering-Back Classes and learn to assert yourself generally. Reading self-help books like this excellent Life Guide will help to restore your self-esteem. When you feel ready to leave the refuge and embark on new relationships, try to find somebear smaller than yourself, then you need never be battered again."

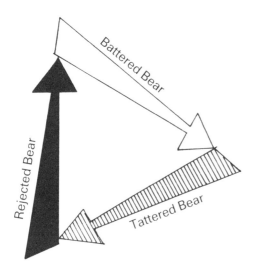

The Vicious Triangle

MINORITY MARATHON

Run for Your Life

Being a member of a minority group has its disadvantages. Being a bear is bad enough; being a Gay Bear, a Single-parent or Disabled Bear, a Koala or a Polar Bear causes overwhelming problems and can lead to grave psychological disorders.

If the Powers-That-Be would but use their imagination a little and put themselves inside a Koala's skin for a moment, they might realize just how they are perpetuating the cycle of deprivation amongst Minority Bears.

For example, it is SCANDALOUS that Koalas cannot attend the Opera because they are unable to use the toilet facilities now provided at Covent Garden. Koalas have come along by leaps and bounds in recent years but they can't be expected to learn everything at once. All that the authorities would need to supply in order for them to be able to visit the Opera is a little patch of earth and a Eucalyptus Tree, and Koalas could drink at the Fountain of Culture, bathe in the Sweet Notes of *La Traviata,* and let the Powerful Voice of *Aida* flush over them.

SUCH DISCRIMINATION MUST BE EXPOSED!

Unless Minority Bears can organize themselves to DEMAND equality in all things — and the facilities to enable them to do this — they will continue to be second class citizens, missing out on the really important things in life.

Instead of diffusing their efforts with their individual organizations and aims, Minority Bears should join forces to fight for a single goal. A Union of Gay Pandas for Half-Price Awaydays, Single-Parent Teds Against Peashooters, Punk Polars in Favour of Koala-Bashing — and all those other well-meaning self-help groups — would be able to compel the Authorities to allow them to participate in THE LONDON MARATHON. Once this Bastion of the Privileged Classes is opened to all-comers, all the doors will be flung wide for Minority Bear.

It's up to YOU. It will be a Marathon Effort, but if it brings with it Free National Health Porridge, a Gay, Single-Parent, Disabl-ed, Koala TV Channel and the Minority Bear Income Supplement, it will be well worth it. So, the message is "Slip into your trainers and start Running for your Life!"

NEW AGE BEAR

Fulfil Your Bear Potential

So you're fit, active and cholesterol-free. You feel like a powerhouse of vitality and untapped energy. But what are you going to do with this well-oiled, finely tuned piece of machinery?

You're going to use it to fulfil your BEAR POTENTIAL! You're going to transform it into a NEW AGE BEAR!

New Age Bear kowtows to no one. He is his own bear, confident and secure in his Roots, he looks forward to a future of unlimited possibilities. He is ready to grab all life has to offer — wealth, happiness, total fulfillment.

But all this isn't going to come to you on a plate. You are not going to be offered a top job as a Captain of Industry unless you learn to project yourself. You must acquire AGGRESSIVENESS SKILLS in order to grab what you want from life.

It's going to be a tough climb up a slippery ladder. You will have to overcome deep-seated prejudices against bears. With your new confidence you will realize that these prejudices are not because you are an inferior furry toy, but are real fears that if bears are let out of the cupboard they will challenge traditional authority; that bears are, in fact, superior beings!

To become a New Age Bear you will have to jump into the mainstream of life — it's no good sitting on the bank dabbling your toes in the water. You will need a network of supportive like-minded bears to help you on your way. Two bears are better than one; ten bears are unbeatable. Once on the inside you must use your influence to bring about positive discrimination in favour of bears. For centuries its been "jobs for the boys"; in the New Age its "jobs for the Bears"! It doesn't matter how lowly these position may be — office mascot or company logo — just fill the place with bears until you are in a position to take over.

AGGRESSIVENESS SKILLS

Claw Your Way to the Top

★ If the boss ignored you and failed to promote you at work, would you cry quietly in a corner, or bite his ankles?
★ If a colleague stroked your ears or patted you on the nose, would you cringe with embarrassment, or throw him over your shoulder?
★ If the milkman asked for two weeks money when you thought you paid him last week, would you pay up meekly, or floor him with a left hook?

If you would have taken the former action in any of these cases you need training in Aggressiveness Skills.

To join the mainstream and become a New Age Bear you will have to cope with just such situations. If you let yourself be trampled on you deserve to be ignored. You must get yourself noticed and the only way to do this is by NAKED AGGRESSION.

Naked aggression is not easy. It means knowing what you want and being prepared to do anything to get it. It's no good being squeamish. You must overcome your natural reticence and good manners. Pinching, biting, scratching, fur-pulling, telling bear-faced lies: all are fair weapons in the armoury of New Age Bear. After years in the nursery, bears will have to be twice as assertive as anyone else if they're going to make it to the top —

they will need to learn guerrilla warfare techniques to break down the enemy and smash traditional prejudices.

This is why you need to join the
EVERYBEAR NAKED AGGRESSION SEMINAR
Here you will learn how to:
● Go into the attack when anyone speaks to you
● Barge into the front of queues, regardless of protest
● Say "Gimme" instead of "Please"
● Throw hot coffee over the boss when he asks you to do anything
● Demand equal rights at your workplace — a rest room for your "bear problems" and a free crêche for your cubs.

Our Aggressiveness Training Workshop will show you that self-defence is old hat for the modern bear. It will teach you to combine your newly acquired fitness and stamina with split-second reflexes so that you can attack where it hurts.

Join our Aggressiveness Programme today.

I would like to learn how to do Naked Aggression. Please enrol me in your Naked Aggression Seminar.

Name ....

Address ....

....

Label No. ....

59

BEARS AT THE TOP
We Meet Some Bears Who Have Made It

Janet — *Media Personality*

There have always been some opportunities for bears in broadcasting, though mostly in children's programmes. But Janet has shown that bears can make it to the top in the media. At first glance it would appear that the cards were stacked against her in her attempt to break into the Big Time. Something of a Minority Bear — a minority of one — she could have stayed in the cupboard and kept her mouth closed. But Janet is a bear of courage. Never one to fall back on her looks alone, she used advanced aggressive techniques to the utmost. Mistress of the tactless question and the earth-shattering laugh, she has melted the hearts of millions.

Mishka — *International Sportsbear*

Soviet bears are treated as equals, so Mishka did not have to overcome the prejudices that face bears in this country. Although the rest of the world was surprised when a bear was appointed Organizer of the Moscow Olympics, it was accepted as quite normal by Muscovites. Mishka has not rested on his laurels. Rumours that he was forced to retire to his dacha when the Games received bad publicity in the West are unfounded. He is merely keeping a low profile. As "Cultural Attaché" at a Soviet Embassy "somewhere" he is the first bear in the world to enter the diplomatic service.

Germaine — *Ursinist Philosopher*

We must never forget Germaine, for it was she who opened our eyes to our unbearable situation. *The Bears' Room, Socks and the Single Bear,* and her seminal work of supreme sociological significance, *Fur is an Ursinist Issue,* are the very foundation of the modern Bear Lib Movement.

Although few bears today remember her name, she still wields considerable influence as the Professor of Ursine Studies at the Eleanor (née Teddy) Roosevelt College at Minnesota. From her luxury Ivory Tower she guides the bear activists of tomorrow and prepares young teds for the struggle ahead.

Aristotle Brunassis — *Billionaire Boatowner*

Born to humble peasant parents on a wooded hillside in Greece, Aristotle was a precocious cub whose itch to hit the bigtime soon showed itself when he cornered Woodland honey stocks in World War II, shipping it to rationed bears all round the pond. He invested his profits in more boats and was a honey millionaire at 21.

He is never seen without a beautiful bear on his arm and has been married 17 times. Now semi-retired, he still supervises the movements of his fleet of boats. He is living proof that if you grasp the opportunity, you can make it too.

EXECUTIVE HABEAR TAT

Life Enhancing Investments for the Socially Mobile Bear

PROBLEMS WITH THE PORRIDGE?

Too hot? Too cold? Too lumpy? Too salty?

Now you can cut out the waiting and
get perfect porridge every time with

THE DIGITAL PORRIDGEMADE

Just pour in the oats and water before you
go to bed and set the digital clock radio alarm
and next morning you will awake to the
sound of soft musak
AND PERFECT PORRIDGE

PM4258 PORRIDGE MAKER £29.95

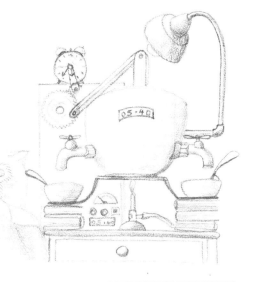

Stop that itch and save a Panda with an

ETHNIC BAMBOO BACKSCRATCHER

Made by Pandas in the Third World.
Every one you buy represents a
weeks food for a Panda.

BS2874 PLASTIC BACKSCRATCHER (Saffron Walden) £4.95

Want a low-cholesterol fat but hate the plastic cartons?

Grace Your Table with a

CERAMIC POLYUNSATURATED
MARG CARTON COVER

Crafted by the skilled potters of Hounslow,
this beautiful piece of China is made to look like REAL BUTTER
Invest in your future: Invest in a ceramic marg carton cover!

PMC8723 POTTERY £9.95

62

Smell like a REAL BEAR
and arouse PRIMEVAL PASSIONS!

GRIZZLY SPLASH-ON

Combines the Earthy Dampness of Ancient Forests
with the Glandular Excretions of the Grizzly.
A UNIQUE EXPERIENCE for You and your Mate!

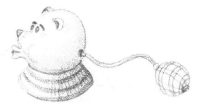

GS7931 SPLASH £15.95

TIME FOR A JAR?

Any time is HONEY time with the

DIGITAL CUT-GLASS HONEY DECANTER

Its microchip technology tells you when the sun is
over the yardarm in NEW YORK — SAN
FRANCISCO — HONOLULU — DELHI —
POTTER'S BAR.

Ideal gift for "retiring" executives.

DCGHD 7932 GLASS JAR £49.95

BOOKS DO FURNISH A ROOM

so furnish *your* den with the

WORLD'S GREATEST CLASSICS

on

REAL SLIMITEX BOOK-SPINE WALLPAPER
with integral shelving

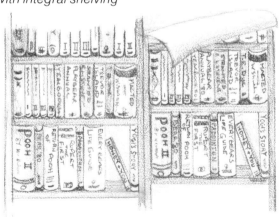

BSW 9348 CLASSICS £9.95 per roll

HOUSEBEARS' CHOICE

Fulfilment through Housework

Not all bears have what it takes to make it to the top in the world of commerce and business and some do not even want to try. There are still a few homely teds around who have a primeval urge to furnish their dens and procreate with regularity. If home and motherhood are your choice there is no need for you to be ashamed. You are free to choose your own lifestyle and you will have to ignore those bear activists who try to denigrate the role of housebear and mummy.

So, if you have decided that marriage and motherhood are for you, remember that housework can be just as fulfilling and rewarding as any other kind of activity. Hoovering the shag pile can be just as excitingly challenging as Grand Prix racing; scrubbing the lino tiles as exhaustingly satisfying as winning the Marathon; mopping up sick as colourfully creative as abstract painting. It all depends on the way you approach the task.

All those career bears on the 8.45 commuter train are probably jealous of your freedom to choose what to do with your day: Shall I dress baby bear in blue or yellow today? Would daddy bear like liver or sweetbreads for supper tonight? Shall I go to the cash-and-carry this morning or this afternoon? Or shall I have just one more tiny spoonful of honey to calm my nerves? The choices are varied and stimulating.

If you have taken the housebear choice, don't hide your light under a bushel. When career bears at parties ask you what you do, don't hang your head and say "I'm only a housebear"; stand up straight and declare "I'm managing director of a little family concern, I'm a food technologist, a comestibles purchasing officer, and a machine room supervisor in my spare time".

SO YOU'RE GOING TO BE A MUMMY BEAR?

Every Bear's Guide to Cubbirth

Have you carefully considered all your options — and rejected Fame and Fortune? Do you *still* long for a "home" and "family"? Well, who is to say you're wrong? If you have opted for housebeardom, then becoming a mummy bear will probably be the most exciting experience of your life and you will want to do it properly! You must make thorough preparations for this ultimate sensation.

Preparing for Cubbirth
Long before you start your cub you will have made sure that your body is a fit place for your "little darling" to grow in. You will have followed the advice in our Fitness Workshop and be in tip-top physical condition. You will have said "goodbye" to all toxic substances and unhealthy practices (see p.39) — play safe and stick to Kapok and Perrier water. Have regular check-ups with your GP and do not start your Tiny Ted until Doctor gives you the go-ahead. Take note: if you are not a fit bear, you are not fit to bear a cub.

What Happens to Your Body
When your cub first starts to grow you will not notice much change in your body. Gradually your tummy will get fatter and fatter — and fatter. Of course, this also happens if you've been overdoing the K-Pok Diet. If you're not sure, lay off the fibre for a bit and if you get even fatter, then . . . you're going to be a Mummy Bear! Congratulations!

10 WEEKS At first your cub is just an assortment of bits and pieces floating around in your tummy, but it has all the parts that go to make up a basic little bear. This is the time you have to be especially careful, for any upset in your system can cause these parts to join together wrongly — such faults can only be corrected by cosmetic surgery after birth.

20 WEEKS Now the parts are connected and only await the arrival of face, fingers and toes.

40 WEEKS Teddy is Ready . . . and raring to go!

30 WEEKS Your cub is now perfectly formed but it needs to grow a little before it is ready to enter the world.

Anti-natal Care

All expectant mummies *must* attend their local Anti-natal Clinic. No one really knows why, but regular periods of sitting in bleak waiting rooms for many hours at a time are essential for mummies-to-be and your Anti-natal Clinic should provide excellent facilities for this. While you are there you could let a doctor (any old doctor will do) have 30 seconds of your time — they may not always show it, but doctors are really terribly interested in you and your cub.

Relaxation Classes

Daddy bears should try to attend Relaxation Classes as they tend to get over-excited when their cub is being born. Here they will also learn how to bathe and change their offspring and make themselves generally useful around the house after the "big event". They will also have the opportunity of discussing their problems and worries with other daddies. Mummies may also find Relaxation Classes useful. Then again, they may not.

THE JOY OF CUBBIRTH

Some Intensely Meaningful Cubbirth Experiences

As with all other aspects of your life, you must make sure that your cubbirth is an intensely meaningful experience. It should be an emotional watershed in your life that you will be able to discuss with other mummies, and anyone else who will listen, for many years to come.

There are many exciting cubbirth methods available and you should investigate them all before you decide on the one that is right for you. Here are just a few stimulating experiences to give you an idea of the range of fulfilling sensations available.

Dr Growly Mick Read's Heavy Breathing Method

Dr Mick Read's well-tried method of Natural Cubbirth (so-called because the only equipment called upon is a "natural" sponge and "natural" water) is based upon the theory that if you learn an intricately complicated pattern of breathing, to be carried out when your cub is being born, you will be so involved in trying to remember which breathing level you are supposed to be on that you will forget about any minor discomfort the birth might be causing. Daddy bears are also involved in this method — they must stand by ready to stuff a wet sponge in your mouth when things get really tough. Just follow the simple diagram below and you won't feel a thing.

Dr Lebear's Hot Bath Method

This chic new birth method is all the rage in Gay Paree and is ideal for the Bear of Taste! Dr Lebear believes that what cubs really like best are hot baths, dark rooms, and Richard Clayderbear records. So when you think your cub is on his way, fill the bath with lovely warm water, wind up the gramophone, and put on a truly unique Clayderbear double album (and remember these are not available from your record shop, so order well in advance of B-day). Now you just turn off the lights and wait for Little Ted to emerge into the lovely dark, damp atmosphere with a virtuoso piano accompaniment.

Computer Birth

If you are a technologically minded teddy bear you may like to try the latest totally safe and sterile computer birth techniques. These are available at all large hospitals, or if you plump for a home confinement, you could plug a Digital Audio Visual Cub Monitoring and Delivery Program into your ZX 81 and your cub will be induced, monitored and delivered shrink-wrapped at the flick of a switch.

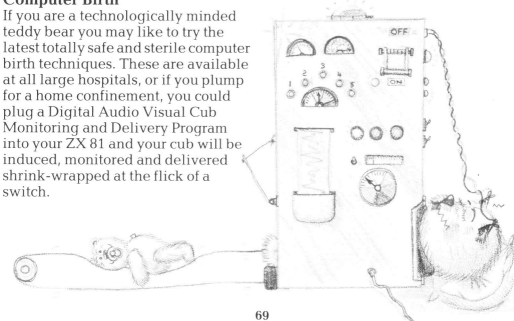

AFTERBIRTH
The Joys of Parenthood

The ecstasy and the agony are over; you are now the proud owner of a cuddly, furry, little bundle of joy. New mummy and daddy bears will find that their lives are completely transformed. Life after birth is a series of stimulating challenges, and the first hurdle is post-cubal depression.

Post-cubal Depression

This is a completely normal hormonal change that has nothing to do with the fact that you are only getting an hour's sleep a night, that you're stuck at home all day with a screaming baby, or that daddy bear only grunts when you try to hold a stimulating conversation of an evening. PCD is absolutely nothing to worry about. Most mummies get it and many recover completely once their little ones have grown up and left home.

Tedling Rivalry

It is unfair on your tedling to bring him up as an only cub. Tedlings need the companionship of brothers and sisters and the cut and thrust of real family life to develop their full potential and enjoy a fulfilled and happy cubhood. You will probably find that your first cub is very jealous when Number Two arrives and he may try to murder it. Make sure that Number Two is well protected at all times. Number Three will probably be jealous of both One and Two and want to take part in all their activities. This will make One and Two very annoyed and they will try to rub him out. Once you are on to Four or Five you will just have to let them get on with it and work out their own pecking order. Your role will be that of referee, merely ensuring that dangerous fouls do not end in excessive blood letting. This tedling rivalry should end when your cubs reach cuberty.

Cuberty and Cubolescence

When your tedlings reach cuberty they will stop fighting amongst themselves and will turn on you. They will reject everything you stand for and behave in ways that are a total anathema to you. The secret of dealing with the cubolescent is *Negative Example.* If you sniff glue at the breakfast table, then your cubolescent will be outraged and disgusted by glue; if you get paralytically drunk every night, then your offspring will never touch a drop; if you play thundering heavy rock all day, then he'll turn to Chopin and Brahms. You may find that setting a negative example is at times rather exhausting, but remember, cubo - lescence lasts only seven years and after that you will be free of your healthy, teetotal paragon. You will be able to congratulate yourself on a job well done.

IS EVERY BODY HAPPY?

Picnic Time for Teddy Bears

If you go down in the woods today,
You're sure of a big surprise.
If you go down in the woods today
You'd better go in disguise,
For Every Bear that ever there was
Will gather there for certain because
Today's the day the Teddy Bears have
their picnic.

Every Teddy Bear who's been good
Is sure of a treat today.
There's lots of marvellous things to eat
And wonderful games to play.
Beneath the trees where nobody sees
They'll hide and seek as long as they
please,
'Cos that's the way the Teddy Bears
have their picnic.

Picnic time for Teddy Bears,
The little Teddy Bears are having a
  lovely time today.
Watch them, catch them unawares
And see them picnic on their holiday.

See them gaily gad about,
They love to play and shout –
They never have any cares.
At six o'clock their Mummies and Daddies
Will take them home to bed
Because they're tired little Teddy Bears.

ENJOYING YOUR RETIREMENT

An Active Old Age

New Age Bear never grows old. By keeping fit and active, senior bears can stay youthful, healthy and fulfilled till their dying day. It is a foolish bear who gives up on retirement to potter in the garden and relax over a pint with old cronies and fond memories. You should be out there with the young ones showing them you can still run a marathon in record time, do one-armed handstands on your windsurfer, and disco dance till dawn, preferably all on the same day. Many "Retirement Homes" provide excellent facilities for all kinds of sports and you should take full advantage of them.

BEARBLIOGRAPHY

Roots

Bearwatching by Desdemona Morris
Desdemona's first book since his "little op"
shows all the old flair. *Bearwatching* sheds
new light on instinctive bearhaviour.

The Bear Wombat by Desdemona Morris
Are we just cuddly wombats? asks Ms Morris.

Creations, vol 1, *Make Your Own Soft Toys*
by Victor Frankenbear and The Singer
Sewing Machine Co.

Was E.T. a Ted? by Erich von Furrykin
Von Furrykin's theory of our extra-terrestrial
origins.

Ursine Imagery in Shakespearean Tragedy
by Marilyn Frog
Prof. Frog has discovered that Shakespeare
used the word "bear" 47 times in his
Tragedies.

Hitler's Bear's Diaries Edited by Huge
Teddy Roper
An authenticated manuscript found behind
the lavatory cistern in East Berlin
Public Library.

All Colour Book of Bears of the Third Reich
by Sydney L. Bayer
Lots of nice pictures of nasty bears.

Fitness Workshop

*How to Prevent Horrible Things Happening
to Your Body* by The Bear Health Advisory
Council
Prevention is better than two years on the
waiting list for a cure.

*The One and Only Truly Amazing
K-©Pok Diet* by Tawdry Bearton
© The letter K© is the copyright of Parrot

Paperbacks and may not be reproduced in any
form without prior permission of the publisher.

*Getting Even Harder: Massive Muscles in a
Month* by Arnold Schwarzentedder
Advanced fluff pumping techniques.

The Black Forest Diet by Judy Bearzel
The diet that transformed the wealthy
inhabitants of the Black Forest is now
available to anybear (who can afford the
book and lots of gateaux). Yes! Eat as much
cake as you like and you too will look like
the lovely Judy.

Bear Beautiful

The Omo Book of Health and Beauty
Wash that muck right out of your fur and
deep- cleanse your way to a beautiful body.

Learn the beauty secrets of the stars with:

Pooh's Guide to Health and Beauty
Yogi's Guide to Health and Beauty
Sooty's Guide to Health and Beauty
Big Ted's Guide to Health and Beauty
Little Ted's Guide to Health and Beauty

Rupert's Guide to Health and Beauty
Roger Q. Bear's Guide to Health and Beauty
etc, etc, etc.

Medical Matters

Everything Your Doctor Wouldn't Tell You Even If He Knew the Answer by Baire Rayner
Fortunately, Baire knows all the answers.

The Pop-Up Book of Open Heart Surgery by Dr Jonathan Growler
Everybear's favourite media medico brings you the first ever do-it-yourself guide to this complex branch of surgery. Its unique use of moving parts shows clearly how to perform every heart operation from inserting a pacemaker to complete transplants.

Living with Athlete's Foot by NAFF (National Athlete's Foot Foundation)
See also *The Complete Naff Guide.*

Are You Mental?

Collecting Exotic Beer Mats A Connoisseur's Guide.

Overmanning on the Bosphorus Ferry by Abdul Istanbear, Institute of Oriental Studies.

Stress Therapy by Dr Ephraim Zimblebear
Bottle up those problems and increase your nervous tension – this is the message from the West Coast for the 1980s.

The Metropolitan Guide to Naked Aggression by The "Metro" Experts
For those bears who haven't the energy to make it to Metro Magazine's "Naked Aggression Workshops".

Bear Harassment at Work N.U.B. Working Party Report
The National Union of Bears have at last exposed the degrading treatment bears suffer at their work places.

Habear tat Catalogue
Even window shopping costs money at Habear tat.

Housebear's Choice

101 Things to Do with Porridge by The Rolled Oats Marketing Council
Some truly amazing porridge-based activities.

The Working Bear's Guide to Picnics and Packed Lunches by Tony Tupperbear
Short cuts to picnic planning for the busy bear.

Free Fall Parachuting and other Pastimes for the Over 80's by Miriam Stopbeard
Life begins at 79 for Miriam.

USEFUL ADDRESSES

Fluffonic Irrigation Services,
31B Mafeking Road,
Hackney.

Gay Koala Switchboard,
Night Lines,
The Telephone Exchange,
London EC4.

Hunnyholics Anonymous,
Sticky Row,
Beeston,
Notts.

Ken Livingstone,
County Hall,
London.

National Cubbirth Trust,
Pooh Corner,
Teddington.

Single Parent Panda Collective,
The Zoo,
London.

INDEX

This was going to be the
most comprehensive
index ever compiled but I
ran out of space. Sorry.